Making Ordinary Moments EXTRAordinary

Parenting Moment by Moment

BECCA GUNYON, MCC

WESTBOW PRESS
A DIVISION OF THOMAS NELSON
& ZONDERVAN

WestBow Press books may be ordered through booksellers or by contacting:

WestBow Press
A Division of Thomas Nelson & Zondervan
1663 Liberty Drive
Bloomington, IN 47403
www.westbowpress.com
844-714-3454

ISBN: 978-1-6642-8581-1 (sc)
ISBN: 978-1-6642-8580-4 (e)

Print information available on the last page.

WestBow Press rev. date: 12/16/2022

Thankful to all the students I have counseled; each of them taught me what they long for in their relationship with their parents.

Thankful to my husband, Dan, who encourages me to write every day.
Thankful for my children, Owin, Addi, Eben, JohnE, and Anden.
Thankful for each member of my family, Gunyon, Owings, and Tuiasosopo.
Thankful to Westbow Publishing for being so wonderful to work with.
Thankful to Lexie Fish for editing.
Thank you, Lord's Way Ministries and The Way Counseling (established 2000).

CONTENTS

INTRODUCTION

As parents, we want to get it right. We desire to cultivate thriving relationships with our children and teens. Much of our relationship with our kids is built in those seemingly ordinary moments. How we live our moments determines the health of our relationships. Creating an atmosphere in our home that allows our kids and teens to grow into adults who give life to the world around them is so rewarding. We can instill honor, kindness, faith, respect, service, and love in our children's lives. These qualities, when lived out in their adult lives, will enrich our own lives in the future. How we choose to live our moments with our kids can build a strong bond that will stand the test of time. We are parenting for today and for tomorrow! One of the best gifts we can give our kids is an enjoyable relationship with us; this helps them grow into adults who give life to the world around them. We can make ordinary moments EXTRAordinary!

Twenty plus years of counseling adolescents created a close-up view of students' hearts, thoughts, disappointments, hopes, and how they perceive life. A group of students gave me an amazing gift of getting to sit across from them. Each student's perception of life has a direct correlation with their feelings about their life at home and their relationship with each parent. The thought process of adolescents is intriguing. For the last twenty years, each time a teenager mentions their parent, I mentally take note. They are teaching me how to communicate with my own kids and teens. Early on in my counseling career, my biggest win was getting a student and their parents to communicate in love.

Two years after I started counseling, my oldest son was born. Having my own child made me realize at an entirely different level that most—almost all—parents want to get it right!

I started thinking about the teens coming to my office and how I could learn from them. How could I help them in their relationship with their parents? What could I glean about parenting from hearing their frustration, needs, heartache, the root of their struggles?

Every student I had the honor of sitting across from taught me something. These ideas in Parenting Moment by Moment are treasures I was given by listening to teens' thoughts, beliefs, and hearts. Extraordinary relationships are built in ordinary moments. These six themes can help you create a blueprint for growing strong relationships with your children.

Each section is designed to be tailored to your own home and family situation. May these six themes enrich your relationship with your children, teens, and adult children.

Dedicated to my parents,
Jim and Danise Owings,
who love wholeheartedly

"Through skillful and godly Wisdom is a house (a life, a home, a family) built,
and by understanding it is established [on a sound and good foundation],

And by knowledge shall its chambers [of every area] be filled with
all precious and pleasant riches." (Proverbs 24:3-4 AMPC)

THEME 1:

Cultivate the Culture

Culture is created by what's important to us. Whether we realize it or not, our home has a culture. As parents, we are given the gift, and responsibility, to cultivate the culture of our home.

The culture we grow up in generally feels normal to us. Oftentimes, we repeat our "normal." Depending on the culture of our household growing up, we can build on an amazing foundation, or we can repeat negative patterns.

Take a few moments to reflect:

What is the current culture of our home?

_____

_____

_____

_____

_____

_____

_____

_____

_____

What was the culture of my childhood home?

_____

_____

_____

_____

_____

_____

_____

_____

_____

_____

_____

What was the tone used in family conversation (loud, quiet, closed off, passive, kind)?

_____

_____

_____

_____

_____

_____

_____

_____

_____

_____

_____

How did I feel in my home?

_____

_____

_____

_____

_____

_____

_____

_____

_____

_____

Do I want to create for my family the same culture I grew up in? Why or Why not?

_____

_____

_____

_____

_____

_____

_____

_____

_____

_____

_____

_____

Am I repeating the "normal" I grew up in? Is this how I want to parent?

_____

_____

_____

_____

_____

_____

_____

_____

_____

_____

Because culture is created by what's important to us, as parents, we have to decide what qualities we want to cultivate in our children. We can ask ourselves, "What do we want our family to be known for?" After taking an honest look at our current culture, we may want to make changes.

When our oldest three kids were all under the age of six, a lifetime mentor asked me and my husband, Dan, a great question. She said, "What do you want your home to look like now, and what do you want it to look like ten years from now? At first this question felt overwhelming. After thinking about it a while longer, we realized she was empowering us now, while our kids were still young, to shape both the current and future culture of our home.

Questions like that can feel scary, yet self-evaluation is powerful and life-giving. Take a moment and ask yourself the same questions: What do I want to cultivate in our household? What do I want the culture of my home to be?

_____

_____

_____

_____

_____

_____

_____

_____

_____

_____

_____

Creating and growing a culture takes time, just like planting. Over the years I've bought many plants. I always get so excited bringing these bright pops of greenery into my home. I place it in a nice sunny spot, I water it, and then, despite my best intentions, life happens. I get busy or distracted. I forget to water it. It gets scorched by the sun. That happy little plant starts to wither. But, if I reset my intentions, if I move it to a better spot in the shade, if I water it and give it a little more attention, it begins to bloom. I also have a few fake plants in my home, they just sit there, adding greenery. They never grow or change, they lack roots.

Some relationships can feel like they are broken or need mending, yet, there is hope that, with the right attention, they can thrive. Other relationships feel fake or lack depth; without roots to grow, that relationship will never expand or evolve. It will stay stagnant, pretty on the outside, but without any depth or real, personal connection. Looking at the reality of our relationships helps us decide where to start taking steps toward depth and growth.

We can take steps toward growing in our relationship with our spouse and kids. Parenting is made up of moments, not once a year vacations or eating dinner at the same table once or twice a week. We cultivate the culture of our home in the ordinary moments, day after day. Even on the rainy days and the stormy days when life is hard, we get to create pockets of fun, moments of peace, joyful time spent with one another.

The result of cultivating consistently is that an amazing culture grows, unique to each home. Our parenting choices to be loving, kind, wise, and prayerful result in growing enjoyable, thriving relationships with our kids, teens, and adult children.

We are given the amazing gift to create the culture we want to live in by our own choices, moment after moment.

Creating a culture takes self-reflection, first we must face our "real."

Do I enjoy the current culture of our home? Why or why not?

_____

_____

_____

_____

_____

_____

_____

_____

_____

Are there changes I need to make?

_____

_____

_____

_____

_____

_____

_____

_____

_____

When Addi (age 18) and Owin (age 20) were ages three and five, they lived in a constant argument. At one point Owin pushed Addi in the pool, she didn't know how to swim. Another time Addi ran over Owin with her Dora motorized bike. They bickered constantly. We tried to correct them and push them to be kinder to each other. Our efforts were futile until we faced the source of their conflict...us! We had to own it; we were growing a mess.

Year seven of our marriage with three kids under the age of six, Dan and I had to look in the mirror and come to the realization that they were learning all of these bad habits from us! They were modeling our tone, our words, and our attitudes toward one another. This wakeup call was painful and required steps toward improvement on our part. We both had changes to make. Our pattern of blaming each other made matters worse. I was bitter, he was frustrated. There wasn't any big scandal in our marriage, yet our home was not a fun, peaceful, or enjoyable place to be.

We faced our mess and met with a counselor. We worked through books, asked ourselves hard questions, and learned to work together. The change was not instant, yet within months of watching us work on our attitude toward one another, our kids started making progress in changing the way they treated each other.

Figuring out what we wanted the culture of our home to look like took some time to formulate. Dan and I each came up with a list, and then we picked our top five. Both Dan and I wanted our marriage to bless our children. We wanted our home to be a place where each of our kids would want to be, a place of kindness, and a safe haven, somewhere they would learn to serve and give, and where love is the response. The outside world can try to tear us down, we desired for the culture of our home to be a place where we encourage and build one another up. Both of us wanted our children to have a foundation of faith. I wanted my kids, when they became adults, to want to come visit, not because they felt obligated to, but because they truly enjoyed spending time with us and each other. Picturing what the future will look like is powerful! We are not just parenting for today, for we are laying a foundation for our future relationship with our adult children!

As parents, it is our responsibility to make this culture happen. Kids rarely respond with honor and grace unless they are coached in kindness, respect, humility, and unselfishness.

Together, we thought through a few questions about how we wanted to achieve this culture. We created steps to repeat day after day, year after year. Each couple can come up with answers unique to their desired family culture and find their own ways to implement.

Repetition lays a foundation for culture. We compiled this list of what's most important to us. As parents, we agreed on creating this culture and making it our goal in the moments of each day. Here are our top five.

The Culture of Our Home

1. Honor one another and serve others.
2. Home is a safe place. Respect each other's boundaries.
3. Affirm and appreciate each other. Continually foster sibling closeness.
4. Be known for being fun.
5. Faith is the foundation. Prayer is our go-to.

You can create your own list by deciding what's most important to you. While you are brainstorming, it's helpful to make a list of practical, simple, and repeatable "how to's." Fine tuning this list might take time, you may find yourself adding and changing ways to implement.

Here are a few of our steps in how to grow the culture we agreed to create.

1. Honor one another and serve others.

   For our family, honor means: treating each other as special, having a good attitude, and doing more than expected. Kids need repetition and consistency. Dan and I use the same verbiage, so they hear from both parents what honor means. For instance, when asked to do a chore, have a good attitude about completing it! Doing more than expected would mean not only unloading the dishes but loading the dishwasher with dishes in the sink. Why? Because this treats mom or dad as special.

   We can model and create an attitude of looking for a way to bless someone else or serve. In the *Choose Life to the Fullest* Series, I end each daily devotion with a simple question "Who can I give life to today?"

   If we raise kids and teens who are giving life to someone each day, their focus shifts to thinking about ways they can bless others instead of thinking about themselves.

2. Home is a safe place. Respect each other's boundaries.

   For us, this means a few things. When respecting each other's boundaries, "Stop" means stop! We joke a lot in our home, but name calling and belittling one another is not acceptable. When someone is unkind, they are corrected. Your tone cannot be hateful or sarcastic. We choose to work through the hard stuff and forgive. With four sons, this one hasn't always been easy. Their tendency at times can be to go "too far" with a joke, because it sounds "funny." Yet, it's not funny to be on the receiving end.

   Great sibling relationships are an amazing gift, but it doesn't just happen. Closeness and kindness take work. As parents, we must teach our kids to think before they speak and act. Tone is key in creating an enjoyable atmosphere. This is our responsibility to model respectful and grace-filled words and attitudes.

3. Affirm and appreciate each other. Continually foster sibling closeness.

   As parents, we create and cultivate opportunities for encouragement. We model encouragement by the way we talk to our kids. Our children and teens are always watching to see how we respond, how we treat our spouse, and how we uplift others. If we are constantly complaining, rude, sarcastic, or belittling, they will follow our example. Kindness and affirmation are learned skills that we choose to cultivate.

   Here is a fun way to start giving encouragement: (It involves candy!)

   All seven of us were on a road trip in our blue minivan the first time we tried this. Road trips with five kids can be challenging. Sometimes, you have to resort to bribery to encourage everyone to get along! The rule was, without sarcasm, say something you like about the person on your right. If your comment is positive, you get a piece of candy. Kind words taste good, just like sugar does. The candy and the compliments set a great tone for the rest of the road trip. Who doesn't want candy? And who doesn't love kind and encouraging words spoken over them?

Our kids and teens enjoyed hearing good things from us and their siblings. Randomly, on road trips, holidays, and family time together, we take turns saying one thing we enjoy about the person sitting beside us. After starting this nine or ten years ago, our kids now ask to do this. It may sound silly, but even our older teens enjoy the "compliment game." Everyone wants to hear great things spoken about them, and it strengthens sibling relationships.

Recently we watched "Rise," the film about the Antetokounmpo brothers. The themes of family is forever and sibling closeness were amazing. Playing basketball on travel teams, these brothers shared shoes without complaining or arguing. Despite having to share, they were each other's biggest fans. Having the support and encouragement of siblings is one of the greatest gifts we can give our kids, teens, and adult children.

4. Be known for being fun.

We wanted our home to be FUN! Fun means making ordinary moments EXTRAordinary!

Home can be an inviting place where our kids love to be. As parents, we cultivate this! What do you want the atmosphere of your home to be? Is a perfectly neat home, with all the chores done and everything in its place important to you? Or would you rather everyone enjoy being home?

It's okay to want a clean home, but sometimes you have to let the little things go. Kids are messy. Spills happen. Teenagers break things. Having a fun home requires a lot of laughter, forgiveness, and understanding.

We can teach our kids to respect property, but they are still going to accidentally break things, and showing grace is so important. As parents, our attitude creates a fun culture, or a stressful culture.

Ways to make the ordinary moments EXTRAordinary:

Under age 10: going on bike rides, playing with sidewalk chalk, balloons on random days, and silly adventures are fun. When my five were all under age 11, we loved to go "park hoppin." We would spend 15 minutes at a park and then hop back in the car and go to the next one on our list!

Older elementary kids: having friends over (even if we're tired), baking cookies, going to get ice cream, or on little adventures one on one.

Teens: having a house with food, fun games, and where noise is allowed. This doesn't mean being okay with wild parties, it just means kids are welcome and noise is okay. Teens are usually loud and need a place to just hang out and have fun. If you make your home the place where your kids want to invite their friends, then you know exactly where they are and don't have to worry about them getting into trouble.

5. Faith is the foundation. Prayer is our go-to.

We wanted our kids to understand that our underlying *why* is our faith! Creating a foundation in Biblical truth and prayer will set you up for success for the rest of your life. There is no such thing as comfortable Christianity for us as parents. We must bring God and Scriptural truths into everything. We are shaping foundations, we are teaching our kids where to run to when they are hurting, and Who to thank when they are celebrating. Everyone is searching for truth and our kids and teens need a foundation that will sustain them always, not something that will fill a hole or void for only a short period of time.

Invite Jesus into everything when they are little. It will model how to live in relationship with our Heavenly Father all the time, not just on Sundays and not just when we sit down to eat dinner. We can pray for ambulances when we hear the siren, thank God for painting the sky such beautiful colors, and teach them to put on the armor daily (for more, read Ephesians 6). When they are in elementary school, teach them verses and Bible stories. In middle school, we can encourage them to build a faith of their own by sharing our faith and our struggles with them, and by praying together. We can bring God into conversations even when our kids are in high school and college. He is our why. We can end a call with our college age kids or adult kids by saying, "What can I be praying for you?" We can help our kids know that Jesus loves them completely and help them embrace that love every day.

We can live out our own, personal faith by the way we treat our kids, spouse, and others around us!

We can ask ourselves:

What culture do I want to create in my home?

_____

_____

_____

_____

_____

_____

_____

_____

_____

_____

What character qualities do I want to cultivate in my children?

_____

_____

_____

_____

_____

_____

_____

_____

_____

_____

How will these character qualities become the culture in our home?

_____

_____

_____

_____

_____

_____

_____

_____

_____

_____

_____

What is the standard of communication in our home? (Do we communicate with kindness, honor, and love?)

_____

_____

_____

_____

_____

_____

_____

_____

_____

_____

Does the way I communicate to my spouse model how I want my kids to talk to me and their siblings?

_____

_____

_____

_____

_____

_____

_____

_____

_____

_____

What can I do to start improving the way I communicate?

_____

_____

_____

_____

_____

_____

_____

_____

_____

_____

What do I want our family to be known for?

_____

_____

_____

_____

_____

_____

_____

_____

_____

_____

Culture is created by what is important to us. Our home has a culture. If we aren't enjoying our culture, we can make changes. As parents, we are given the honor, gift, and responsibility to cultivate the culture of our home.

Daily, we are cultivating the culture of our home.

We can start creating a new atmosphere at any moment!

THEME 2:

Create Thriving Relationships

Each child and teen desires to experience closeness with their parent in an authentic way!

Having healthy and meaningful relationships with each of our kids and teens can feel out of reach at times, but with a few small shifts in our thoughts or behavior, we *can* build strong relationships with our children. Close knit relationships don't happen by chance, it's the small and intentional moments throughout parenting that create thriving relationships between you and your kids. The challenge might be determining where to start. For most of us, life seems to be moving too fast and there is so much to get done. Even in the busy swirl of life, what are practical "how-to's" of developing a relationship with each of our children or teens?

Take a moment to ask yourself:

What does a healthy relationship look like?

_____

_____

_____

_____

_____

_____

How does my child feel about me? How do I feel about each of them?

_____

_____

_____

_____

_____

_____

_____

_____

_____

_____

Our thoughts about those we love affect our relationship—for good, or for bad. We have the incredible opportunity to transform relationships by changing our thoughts about our kids and our spouse, and the way we view parenting. We get to choose what we think about those around us!

"We live out our thoughts." (Gunyon, 2019)

> If you are committed, you can select your thoughts and thereby shape your life here on earth into something spectacular. The alternative is to give up this freedom and live a life of mediocrity dominated by uncertainty and suspense. (Newberry, 2007)

This is true about all relationships. We live out our thoughts and it affects the way we perceive others—in the past, today, and tomorrow.

What do I think about each person in my home? (Include thoughts on your spouse and each child or teen.)

_____

_____

_____

_____

_____

_____

_____

_____

_____

_____

Do I think well of those I am doing life with? Have I considered how my thoughts affect our relationship?

_____

_____

_____

_____

_____

_____

_____

_____

_____

_____

What do I think my spouse and children think about me?

_____

_____

_____

_____

_____

_____

_____

_____

_____

_____

_____

_____

1. The first adjustment in our thought life involves our thoughts about who we live with:

Our first thoughts, from the moment we wake up, fuel how we will act for the rest of the day and who we will be to everyone around us. Each morning, focusing on one amazing character quality in our spouse and each of our kids fuels our relationship and attitude towards them. When we focus on the good, it's reflected in our tone, our attitude, our words, and our actions; this ultimately shapes our relationship. In contrast, if we focus on the negative and think belittling or demeaning thoughts about our kids or spouse it will come out in our tone and the way we treat our family members.

For example, if your teen forgets to take out the trash, you might think, "They always forget, they are so lazy! How are they going to function in life being so irresponsible?!"

To shape our thought life toward positivity, we can adjust our internal dialogue to, "My teen forgot to take out the trash, it's frustrating, yet he or she was up late doing homework." We can continue on the positive track of our thought life by adding in other positive perceptions about our children. For example, "They are so kind to others and are working really hard in their sport or activity. I wonder if there is something going on that is causing them to forget about this chore, I've asked them to do."

The situation didn't change, but when we give a grace-filled explanation, it takes us down a much better path, one where we choose to think well of our children. Every thought we have, we can take captive and turn it to a positive truth. This doesn't mean we let our teen off the hook of doing chores, and it doesn't mean there isn't a consequence for their action, or lack of action, but our tone and word choice will be different if we are thinking well of our kids.

What annoys me about my spouse and each of my kids?

Does this affect the way I treat them? How?

_____

_____

_____

_____

_____

_____

_____

_____

_____

_____

Our thoughts shape our relationships. Negative thoughts about those we live with taint the purity of relationships.

Do you have a loud child? They might talk loudly, chew loud, move loud, or even just breathe loud. Have you ever been in the car or on a trip where you keep bottling up your emotions and feelings until suddenly you hear yourself saying, "I just need everyone to SHUT up!" It seems to come out of nowhere; your response is a level 7 or 8 to a level 3 or 4 issue. Our thoughts all along the way are what take us to these extreme responses to something that probably wasn't a big deal on its own… but with one small thing after another, suddenly it's huge!

Our frustration fuels our response. If we keep our negative thoughts in our head, they can keep spiraling until it feels out of control. You might be someone who shuts down from the chaos, or you might be someone who yells. Neither reaction is going to be helpful to your family or the situation. Instead of trying to keep your thoughts to yourself (until they inadvertently come out anyway), take them captive and address the situation in a positive way. Instead of waiting until you're at a breaking point to tell everyone to, "Just be quiet!" Try taking a deep breath. The thought that was, "All this noise is driving me crazy!" can instead be, "How can I lead my car toward a (quiet) game or kindly correct my child who may not understand how to be noise-considerate?"

Most of us don't realize we are walking around thinking thoughts of frustration toward those we love. When we lose control of our thought life, we are taking steps away from a healthy and thriving relationship and moving toward pain or frustration in a relationship that will eventually need to be repaired.

Alright, so you may be thinking, "How do I start to change my thoughts?"

Regardless of our situation, if we wake up and think about one quality in our spouse and each of our kids that we are grateful for, our attitude will reveal what is going on in our heart. This will follow us the rest of the day… in the carpool line, driving to sports practice, watching them play or perform, making dinner, tucking them in, to late night conversations with our teens. If we believe that these moments are gifts, we will reflect this attitude in our daily life.

We can ask ourselves:

Are the thoughts I wrote about above strengthening or harming my relationships? How?

Do I want to think differently? How do I start?

_____

_____

_____

_____

_____

_____

_____

_____

_____

What is one character quality or strength I can focus on in my spouse and child or teen?

_____

_____

_____

_____

_____

_____

_____

_____

_____

The same character trait that frustrates you might also be one of their strengths if we view it a little differently.

For example:

Owin (my oldest) is very stubborn, yet as an older teen and young adult this quality has served him well. He makes wise choices, even when everyone around him is not. His stubbornness has also made him a great leader.

Eben moves slowly, which can look like rebellion or laziness. However, it's not, he is just methodical. This has translated into him making informed choices instead of rash decisions.

JohnE is loud and full of energy. As a toddler, he was wild. As a middle schooler, he makes people feel special, is kind to everyone, and brings excitement and energy everywhere he goes.

Our thoughts shape our feelings about each person in our family and we live these out. Our attitude in life will be revealed whether we want it to or not. We must be intentional about our thoughts. Something I do every day to be deliberate about thinking one great thought about my spouse and kids is set a reminder on my phone for when I wake up. The *first* thing I do is go to one positive affirmation about my closest loved ones. For example: Dan is loyal, Owin is a leader, Addi is authentic, Eben is wise, JohnE is loving, Anden is strong. My thoughts about each of them affect the way I treat them. I can correct my children in love, wisdom and patience when I am thinking well of them.

Choosing to think about one great quality in the people we love can transform relationships! We can pick one character trait and think about this same quality in our spouse or kids daily for a year.

2. The second thought adjustment requires thinking about our goal.

Knowing our goal is key in staying motivated.

What is my parenting goal?

_____

_____

_____

_____

_____

_____

_____

_____

_____

If a thriving relationship is our goal, we have to constantly remember what culture we are committed to cultivating. Intentionally focusing on our goal helps us build thriving relationships with our kids and teens. Our why and our goal will fuel us when we get frustrated, tired, or want to give up.

One of my biggest motivators has always been that I want my kids to enjoy being with me. I strive to be a person I would want to hang out with. Being the type of parent who I would want to be parented by requires that I think before I speak, sometimes it means I don't speak—it means I ask myself lots of questions and take time for reflection, and it means my response is one I would want to receive.

My goal is for my kids to *want* to hang out with me! I'm still working on it, but EVERYTHING is filtered through this lens.

Take a few moments to reflect:

Do I focus on things that don't matter? Why or Why Not?

_____

_____

_____

_____

_____

_____

_____

What changes do I need to make to focus on what is important?

_____

_____

_____

_____

_____

_____

_____

Do I feel like it's "too late?" Why?

_____

_____

_____

_____

_____

_____

_____

No matter the age of your child, teen, or adult child… It's never too late to grow in relationship! Creating amazing relationships starts with our thought life.

Looking down the road ten or even twenty years, what kind of relationship do I want with my children?

_____

_____

_____

_____

_____

_____

_____

Is the way I am parenting today going to lead to the relationship I hope to have with my children when they are adults?

_____

_____

_____

_____

_____

_____

_____

We all want to "get it right" with our kids. Knowing that each of our children and teens desire an authentic relationship with us motivates us to take daily steps toward a good thought life. As we carefully choose our thoughts, speak life-giving words, and grow in relationship with our kids, God works in us to build a strong foundation. He takes the messy and shapes it into masterpieces.

As parents, we have the choice to focus on the aspects about our children that really matter. The qualities we want them to develop and the relationship we are growing with them is far more important than the small things that might seem big in the moment, but don't matter in the long run. We must decide what is important to us, and what will stand the test of time. Every aspect of life doesn't have the same value. For instance, if our teen serves or volunteers willingly, gives generously, strives in school, and works hard in their extracurricular activities or sports, we probably need to let some little things go. It's okay if they have a messy car or don't put up their laundry.

What do we want to be remembered as: a parent who notices every little thing that our teen misses or messes up, or a parent who encourages them in their wise choices, gifting, and character qualities? As adults, we don't enjoy being scrutinized, so why do we do this to our kids? To have a well-rounded child and teen, we must walk beside them, helping to mold them into who God wants them to be without causing stress or rebellion or requiring perfection.

We can start building great relationships today in our thoughts, the words and tone we use, and by remembering our why. Over time, we will be blessed by developing stronger relationships. Be encouraged, God can take broken relationships and transform them into healthy ones. It is never too late to reach out and start enjoying moments with your child, teen, or even young adult child.

God handpicked us to parent our children, He will empower us with everything we need. Thankfully, God in His goodness works through our mistakes, gives grace, and transforms relationships.

> *"And we know that in all things God works for the good of those who love him, who have been called according to his purpose." (Romans 8:28 NIV)*

THEME 3:

Communicate

Our teens and children want to communicate with us. It may feel easier with your younger children. They want to talk to you, tell you about their day or friends at school, but with our teens it can feel harder to connect. Teens want us (their parents) to have conversations with them. To interact with them, not to interrogate them. To be genuinely interested in what they have to say.

How do we (my kids and I) communicate?

Do my children and teens want to communicate with me? What do we normally talk about?

_____

_____

_____

_____

_____

_____

_____

_____

When my five kids were all under age 10, I started observing the parent-teen relationships around me that were thriving. What was different about those relationships where the parents and teen enjoyed each other?

My observation led me to believe the biggest difference was the communication styles. Cultivating communication always wins over controlling communication. Control for the sake of control stifles relationships.

When my kids were little, I was constantly interviewing parents who had thriving relationships with their adult kids. One mom of two grown daughters told me that in high school, her teen was a 4.0 student, served at church, and was an artist. Despite all that, this mom was constantly telling her daughter how frustrating her messy room was. This was a source of dissension in their relationship until one day, she decided to stop focusing on the messy room, and instead spend more time enjoying who her daughter is. Fifteen years later as a grown woman, her daughter keeps her house immaculate, is a great mom, continues in her art pursuit, and they have a great relationship! They share a close mother-daughter bond that stood the test of time. This mom realized she wanted to cultivate positive communication instead of arguing about the small things that didn't have a lasting impact.

That is what we all want, isn't it? To enjoy our kids when they become adults. Every day we are making investments in the future friendship we will have with our kids. Our communication today matters for our relationship tomorrow.

So where is the miss? So often we get stuck focusing on and talking about the one thing our kids aren't doing well. We are trying to control our teens instead of finding out what is going on in their heart and minds. We are missing the opportunity to continually cultivate a relationship where we can guide and equip them to make their own wise choices.

What can I do to create an atmosphere where my kids want to communicate with me?

Teens want us (parents) to pursue them.

This may look different for each of our teens. Creating a space for my five kids to talk to me and Dan (my husband) is unique to their wiring and preference. Our youngest child is eleven right now, he has always been quiet in the car when everyone is piled in. He waits until he's only with me or Dan, alone in the car, and then talks the entire time! He needs to know his voice has value. My middle teens usually wait to tell me details about their life until they are ready.

Our teens rarely want to talk when we want them to, and sometimes their reaction can feel like rejection. After twenty years of counseling adolescents and hearing their hearts, I am convinced that every student wants their parents to pursue a relationship with them. We must keep pursuing them, they desire to connect with us. Be patient.

Teens do not always connect with us when we are ready, their timing is different than ours.

As parents, we have to decide, do I want this relationship more than…. (Whatever I wanted to do)?

Many times, when it's late at night or when I'm in the middle of something, I feel inadequate or impatient; I really want to do what I want to do. In these moments, I remind myself of my WHY. I want an authentic relationship with my kids, and I want each of them to communicate with me. In this instance of impatience or inadequacy, we can say a simple prayer in our mind, "God give me strength to listen and reply the way You want me to. Guide me."

It may be different in your family, but it feels like my teens always want to talk to me when it's late and I'm tired or I feel like I don't have anything left in me for the day. This is usually the time when my three high school kids tell me their real—what is going on in their heart, mind, and in their relationships. You might not feel like you're ready for it, but you get to lean in and be available for them! Most of the time, they just want to know you're listening.

You may be asking yourself, "How can I get my student to talk to me?"

1. Create an atmosphere of safety. Being available, being patient, and having an approachable tone and demeanor are essential.

2. If we want our kids to talk to us, we need to communicate by using the same tone we want them to use with us. We can ask ourselves, "Am I speaking to my kids in a way I want them to repeat back to me?"

3. Listen before we speak. If we want to know what's going on, we need to stop talking. Listen, pause, ask questions, repeat.
   We might feel like we know all the solutions to their situation, but instead of telling them what to do, it's more effective to ask, "What do you think you should do?" Let them process and wrestle with the answer. If we give our opinion too early, we lose the conversation, and it feels like a lecture. We want our kids to communicate with us, so we have to stop talking and listen, encourage, and choose our words wisely.

4. Be brief. We have about three to five minutes before they stop listening to our advice.

5. One of the MOST important things to keep in mind is to wear our "game face." If our teen tells us something that makes us angry, afraid, shocked, or fearful, we must do our best to keep our emotions to ourselves and resist the urge to react, yell at, or shame them. Asking questions and staying calm will encourage them to keep talking and opening up to us. We may need time to come up with a plan for the next steps or consequences. The situation doesn't need to be fixed or decided on in this moment. Why? Because we want our kids to keep coming to us with all their stories. The good and the bad.

6. Praying with our kids models asking God for help. There have been times when my kids or teenage clients shared hurts and I really didn't know what to say or how to help in that moment. After hearing their heart and asking questions, I say, "This is really hard, I am so sorry you are walking through this. In this moment, I don't know how to help, but I am always here for you." I ask, "Can I pray for you right now?" So far, no one has said no to

this. Inviting the power of Jesus into their situation creates hope. It reminds them that they don't have to carry whatever they are dealing with alone. As we pray with our kids, we are teaching them to pray. (Philippians 4:6-7)

Don't give up! We as parents have so much to say and teach, yet if we listen first then we will learn what is going on in our kid's mind and heart. Listening to them opens the door for them to listen to us. This takes patience, especially if your teen is an introvert, but sometimes, when we least expect it, we will get a meaningful conversation.

Communication will happen if we create an atmosphere where our kids feel loved and safe to share their heart.

Self-Reflection:

Do my kids feel like I'm available for them? When?

_____

_____

_____

_____

_____

_____

_____

Am I patient? Is there one child I'm more impatient with? Why?

_____

_____

_____

_____

_____

Do I have an approachable tone and demeanor?

_____

_____

_____

_____

_____

_____

What does my child or teens' body language reveal about the way they feel about me? What are they trying to communicate to me?

_____

_____

_____

_____

_____

_____

In the middle of a tense moment, do I speak to my kids in a way I would want them to repeat back to me?

_____

_____

_____

_____

_____

_____

If my answer is "no" to any of these questions, how can I start making changes?

_____

_____

_____

_____

_____

_____

_____

_____

Who is a parent I would like to be more like in the way I parent my own kids?

_____

_____

_____

_____

_____

_____

_____

_____

Extra advice on how to communicate about grades, sports, and goals:

When our oldest son started high school, I had a lot of questions on what standard we should set, how to help him get good grades, and what was reasonable to require or ask of him. I asked a wise family minister, Al Causey, who is a parent of thriving adult children, for his advice.

I knew we had five kids to take through this next chapter of high school—standardized testing, goals, dreams, hobbies, even volunteer roles—preparing them to fly as adults, and I wanted to get it right! With this in mind, Dan and I sought wise counsel.

Al explained to me what he and his wife, Debbie, asked of their own kids to help them succeed.

1. What are you capable of?
2. What are your scholastic goals? Why?
3. How can we as parents walk beside you?

These questions can be used in sports, hobbies, and other goals our kids have.

I loved this blueprint, because it is up to our kids to own their own results, not Dan or I to push them. This model was a step of letting go and allowing our children to make their own goals. It gave control to our high school aged children and lessened the opportunity for us as parents to have uncommunicated expectations. Our kids are in charge of their success, but we still get to walk beside them. When one of my kids didn't want to do their homework, I would remind them, "Remember your goals for yourself. How can I help you in this?"

Two of ours have finished high school and one is in upper high school. They own their work and their performance—no pressure from us. This model has worked with all of them and led to the results they hoped they could attain, but most of all, has strengthened our relationship,

My high schooler had a friend ask him, "Don't your parents get mad if you make a bad grade?" He replied, "No, it's my grade, so it's my responsibility to bring it up."

In regard to my teenagers' school, sports, work, what can I change in my tone, my words, and my expectations to enrich our relationship?

_____

_____

_____

_____

_____

_____

_____

What area of my teens' life can I ask these questions and help them own their success, while walking beside them?

_____

_____

_____

_____

_____

_____

_____

"Fathers, don't frustrate your children with no-win scenarios. Take them by the hand and lead them in the way of the Master." (Ephesians 6:4 MSG)

THEME 4:

Continual Affirmation

Our children and teens desire our affirmation. They become what we speak over them.

When our oldest was in sixth grade, his church small group leader, Darren Clark, started telling him that he was a leader. He was the youngest and shortest in his grade and had many reasons why he didn't see himself this way. However, since Mr. Darren spoke this over him, Dan and I followed and started telling Owin, "You are a leader!" Now, at twenty, he became what was spoken over him.

As parents, we get the amazing opportunity to be the echo in our kids' minds. Our kids will believe, live out, and often become what we speak over them. Our words have power over our kids' thought life. "Research shows that 75 to 98 percent of mental, physical, and behavioral illness comes from one's thought life." (Leaf, 2007).

We are given the incredible responsibility to influence our kids' thoughts with our words. The positive affirmations we want our kids to live up to is what we need to constantly repeat and speak over them.

Take a second to reflect:

What words echo in your mind?

_____

_____

_____

_____

_____

_____

_____

_____

Are these words life-giving?

_____

_____

_____

_____

_____

_____

_____

_____

Did someone speak this over you or did life help this word find you?

_____

_____

_____

_____

_____

_____

_____

Do you want this message to echo in your kids' minds?

_____

_____

_____

_____

Imagine what thoughts your kids might be hearing: "You are not enough (socially, athletically, academically). You are overlooked, weird, rejected, don't fit in…" The voice of rejection is cruel! That's why our kids need our voice! Our voice is SO powerful and what we speak over them can be the echo in their minds, battling all of the negativity that kids are confronted with.

Each day, we can speak one life-giving, repetitive phrase to our child and/or teen. By doing this we are telling them, "I love who you are."

Our words become the echo in their minds. We have so many things to say, to teach, to instill, yet this one phrase we repeat over them shapes what they think about themselves. Choosing a phrase to speak daily, both when life is calm and crazy creates a consistent foundation. This also communicates to our children, "My love is not contingent on what you do or don't do, my love for you is based on *who* you are." We might not like our kids' behavior or attitude at times, but we can always show love toward who they are as a person, even if we are correcting or guiding their actions. This also takes away performance-based behavior in our relationship with them. Speaking a phrase of acceptance daily influences their mindset toward God and their view of God's love.

Our repetitive words lay a foundation of our children's identity. Communicating "You are lovable," creates a concrete foundation and further moves them closer to the unconditional love of God. Unconditional love and acceptance can be given to each of our kids as individuals, even if we disapprove of their behavior or action in a moment.

We affirm the character they live by—not the results, "I love how hard you work! You are a great leader. You are kind."

Our words have power! Choosing to speak life-giving thoughts and encouragement over our kids gives them an amazing advantage in their self-confidence and self-worth. Don't underestimate the power of your words as a parent. Speak into our teens who we want them to be! The power of words is beyond our comprehension. Teens cling to words spoken over them. Our words are either life-giving or discouraging.

> Researchers have shown that hurt feelings from words affect the same area in the brain – the cingulate gyrus – as a broken bone or physical injury. So, the old Scottish nursery rhyme of "sticks and stones will break my bones, but words will never harm me" is most certainly not true.
>
> Experts have also found that loving words help heal and rewire this pain. Words are the symbolic output of the exceptional processes happening on micro anatomical, epigenetic and genetic levels in the brain. They contain power to make or break you, your loved ones, your colleagues and your friends. (drleaf.com)

If we want to raise leaders, we can say, "You are a leader. You are wise. God made you strong." Students cling to one or two words, names, or phrases their parents call them and tend to live it out. Even in jest, calling your kid "troublemaker" or "busybody" can have negative effects on their self-image.

A few positive affirmations to speak over your child are: You are brave, a leader, chosen, loved, treasured, special, courageous, a conqueror, strong, created by God with an amazing purpose. Two repeat words in our home are Champion and Treasure (for more, visit championtribe.org and cherishedcircles.org)

What am I currently speaking over my child or teen?

_____

_____

_____

_____

_____

_____

What do I think my child or teen thinks about themself?

_____

_____

_____

_____

_____

_____

_____

What do I want to echo in their minds?

_____

_____

_____

_____

_____

_____

How can I regularly communicate this?

_____

_____

_____

_____

_____

_____

_____

What word or phrase can you speak over your kids every morning?

_____

_____

_____

_____

_____

_____

_____

"When she speaks, her words are wise, and she gives instructions with kindness." (Proverbs 31:26 NLT)

THEME 5:

Construct Boundaries, Guidelines, and Guardrails

Knowing what the boundaries, guidelines, and guardrails are helps to make our kids and teens feel secure. Even though they might resist our regulations, knowing what's expected and where we draw the line creates stability for our children. The underlying goal behind being consistent in our boundaries is to raise kids who we want to hang out with and teens who will grow into adults we enjoy being around and that contribute to the world around them. Every lesson we teach our kids and teens is preparing them for adulthood.

Communicating boundaries and guidelines:

1. State the boundary and guardrails you have decided on.
2. If asked "why?" present the information without being upset at your child or teen for asking.
3. Ask if the boundary is clear.
4. Expect your kids to keep the boundaries and guardrails.
5. Communicate the consequences for not adhering to the boundaries and guardrails, and have a plan to enforce them.

What boundaries, guidelines, and guardrails am I expecting from my kids and teens?

_____

_____

_____

_____

_____

_____

_____

How am I communicating boundaries, guidelines, and guardrails with my children?

_____

_____

_____

_____

_____

_____

_____

Things to remember:

Every time our child's tone or word choice is not respectful, we correct. If you don't like the way your child is communicating to you, slow down and course correct as soon as you can. This might look like saying, "Hey, I know you're frustrated, but it's not okay for you to talk to me like this. Please try again."

We don't yell or be rude back, if we do, we are losing their respect and our authority. We model what we want: strength, respect, kindness, honor, love. We are always training our kids for adulthood. We don't want to raise adults who complain, make excuses, argue with authority, or do a half-way job. We live in a culture of excuses. When given an excuse, remember that excuses don't change the boundary or guideline and there are still consequences.

What tone is my child using with me?

_____

_____

_____

_____

_____

_____

Are my kids modeling my communication? How is my tone and word choice with my children and teens?

_____

_____

_____

_____

_____

Is my child making excuses for their behavior, tone, or actions?

_____

_____

_____

_____

_____

Keep our *why* in mind. Looking 10 or 15 years down the road, remember the goal of having raised young adults who you enjoy spending time with and who want to spend time with you! This can feel exhausting or repetitive but keeping our why in mind will keep us going on those long days and in the difficult moments.

Model the words and tone you want them to use—if your kids and teens are cussing or yelling, ask yourself, "Am *I* yelling at my kids? Are they responding in the way they see modeled, or am I calm and strong when I correct them?"

This is what I've heard from teens. They do not want to be shamed, "shoulded", humiliated, or condemned—this causes anger and rebellion. They do want guidelines and boundaries that make them feel secure. They want to know the rules and the why behind the rules. They are going to test us by pushing on our guidelines.

If we are struggling with this concept, we can choose a person in our life to tell us the hard truth about how we are parenting. Seeking help is brave and, at times, humbling, and it will keep us moving toward our goal. An honest person who is willing to lean in and give the hard feedback of if our kids are respectful and kind, or disobedient, rude, and unenjoyable is a gift!

What if our kids and teens are going to cross over the boundary or break rules, what do we do?

We need a plan, and it helps if both parents use the same plan.

Without anger, frustration, or shame, we talk to them.

1. Ask. Get to the heart, "What led you to _____? Or "Why do you talk to me like this? Are you angry, sad, jealous, bored, do you think the rules are unreasonable?" By asking, we enter into their world and hear their heart.

2. Act. Show them love in action. Say, "I love you and understand life is hard or you are struggling, I'm here for you and will walk through this with you. Yet, because you chose to _____. There are still consequences." Address the behavior you don't like and give a corresponding task or correction. (For example: because you chose to _____, now you have to _____.)

3. Give your kids hope. Ask, "Could you have chosen differently?" Or "How will you do this differently next time?"

   For example: Instead of punching your brother, if you were angry with him, you could have gone into another room, or come and talked to me about it.

4. Remind them we all need God's help. "Can we pray together about this? "Encourage them to invite Jesus into their _____ (frustration, anger, rebellion, disrespect).

5. Keep checking on their heart and helping them work through what they are struggling with.

Can I set guidelines, boundaries, and guardrails and stick to them?

_____

_____

_____

_____

_____

_____

Do I communicate rules and expectations without emotion? How?

_____

_____

_____

_____

_____

_____

What are appropriate consequences if my kids or teens go over the boundary, guideline, or guardrail?

_____

_____

_____

_____

_____

_____

Is my tone, word choices, and communication with my children emotional and shaming? If so, what adjustments do I need to make?

_____

_____

_____

_____

_____

_____

Do I listen to their emotions reflecting love, compassion, and hope? If not, how can I do this?

_____

_____

_____

_____

_____

_____

What is the best way for me to partner with my child/teen and help them make wise decisions?

_____

_____

_____

_____

_____

_____

Am I praying with my kids? If not, am I willing to start?

_____

_____

_____

"Do not be anxious about anything, but in every situation, by prayer and petition, with thanksgiving, present your requests to God. And the peace of God, which transcends all understanding, will guard your hearts and your minds in Christ Jesus." (Philippians 4:6-7 NIV)

THEME 6:

Choose to be Fully Present

Because every child and teen desire an authentic relationship with us, every moment counts! I know what you're thinking, because I thought it too: "We are so busy! How can I make sure I'm connecting with my kids and hearing each of their hearts?"

During a lunch meeting with the Director of Care at North Point Church, as I was seeking parenting advice on how to balance letting my older kids grow and helping them thrive, with my younger ones' activities, and working part-time serving in ministry, she gave me a jewel of wisdom, "Be fully present."

Be fully present. What does this mean? How can I practically be *fully* present in every moment? At first, this can feel overwhelming! In the swirl of life, slowing down enough to be fully present in each moment can be challenging, yet the return on investment in your relationship with your kids is beyond rewarding.

After this conversation, I started asking myself this question, "What does it mean to be present with each one of my children?"

For me, I realized being fully present means embracing moments. Each moment is a gift! Relationships grow in random, seemingly ordinary moments.

Maybe you have thought, "I just need meaningful time to develop a relationship with each of my children. I need to schedule more dates with them or plan our next family vacation." While specially planned on-one-one time and family vacations are great, it's all those in between moments, the seemingly ordinary minutes between the big things that grow an extraordinary relationship!

Small moments with our children and teens sum up their childhood, their memories of growing up. Our experiences with our kids are shaping how we will be remembered. They may not remember all of the things we do, but they will remember how we make them feel.

The majority of moments seem ordinary: in the car, getting ready for school, helping with homework, doing yard work, cleaning the garage, making dinner, or running errands. If we wait for the "big" moments, we will miss countless opportunities to be fully present with our kids in the moments in between. Viewing every moment as a gift allows us to continually develop closeness with our kids.

We can ask ourselves:

What does being *fully* present mean for me?

_____

_____

_____

_____

_____

Am I embracing the seemingly ordinary moments with my kids (in the car, making dinner, helping with homework)?

_____

_____

_____

_____

How can I make ordinary moments extraordinary by my thoughts, tone, words?

_____

_____

_____

_____

_____

Personally, I have found making ordinary moments extraordinary requires me to continually ask myself the question, "How can I be fully present with the person I am with?" Here are a few of my thoughts on what it looks like to be fully present:

- Being fully present means putting my phone down.
- Being fully present means making eye contact.
- Being fully present means asking a follow-up question.
- Being fully present means resisting the temptation to let myself be interrupted by something or someone.
- Being fully present means, at times, dropping what I'm doing to be available for what my kids need.
- Being fully present means responding in a tone I would like to hear.
- Being fully present means enjoying each moment as a gift.
- Being fully present means my spouse or the child/teen who I am talking to is the most important person in the world to me at that moment.
- Being fully present means remembering to play, laugh, and not take life too seriously.

Our time goes so quickly, even if it feels long in the moment.

After counseling teens for twenty plus years and hearing their hearts, I realized each teen wants to be pursued by their parents, even if they do not respond the way that is desired or expected by the parent. I encourage you to join me in making adjustments to be fully present for each member of our family. Although our teens may not respond immediately, in time their response will be a gift to us.

What small change do I need to make this week to be fully present?

_____

_____

_____

_____

_____

What changes do I need to make long term to be fully present?

_____

_____

_____

_____

_____

Digging deeper, what did the in between moments with my own parents look like?

_____

_____

_____

_____

_____

_____

How did this make me feel?

_____

_____

_____

_____

_____

_____

What did I hope for from my parents? How can I give this to my own kids?

_____

_____

_____

_____

_____

_____

During Addi's senior year I took her fun places: weekly Crumble Cookie adventures and monthly lunches. Yet when I asked her about her favorite time with me, she said going to the grocery store together. The ORDINARY! I was trying to create big, memorable moments and she was content doing life with me in those seemingly ordinary moments.

How can I make an ordinary moment with my kids extraordinary?

_____

_____

_____

_____

_____

_____

Looking at each one of my children, when do they enjoy connecting with me most?

_____

_____

_____

_____

_____

_____

May being fully present give you the gift of enjoying the seemingly small moments that will enrich your relationships with each member of your family.

"Rejoice always and delight in your faith; be unceasing and persistent in prayer; in every situation [no matter what the circumstances] be thankful and continually give thanks to God; for this is the will of God for you in Christ Jesus." (1 Thessalonians 5:16-18 AMP)

"...Making the very most of your time [on earth, recognizing and taking advantage of each opportunity and using it with wisdom and diligence] ..." (Ephesians 5:15 AMP)

FINAL REFLECTION

After reading through these six themes, you might be asking yourself, "Is all of this parenting work worth it?" The answer is "YES!" You are one of the most valued influences on the spiritual, relational, mental, and physical wellbeing of your baby, toddler, child, teen, and even adult children. God will empower you to make small shifts in your thoughts, tones, words, and reactions that will have a lifetime effect on your child.

As parents, we want to get it right! While we aren't always going to be perfect, it's never too late to start lovingly pursuing your child. Our family backstory and my passion for sharing this with other parents is because I witnessed a miracle happen in our home with one of our children. A broken relationship grew into a thriving relationship.

This verse, when applied, can transform us into the parents our children and teens need us to be:

> *"I can do all things [which He has called me to do] through Him who strengthens and empowers me [to fulfill His purpose—I am self-sufficient in Christ's sufficiency; I am ready for anything and equal to anything through Him who infuses me with inner strength and confident peace.]" (Philippians 4:13 AMP)*

As we cultivate the culture of our home, think life-giving thoughts about each other, affirm one another, set healthy boundaries and guidelines, and live fully present in each moment, there will still be days we feel tired, lost, or overwhelmed. When these days of feeling defeated hit, I want to share one of my secrets with you: In that overwhelming moment, we can pause, whisper a prayer, take a deep breath and reflect on what it looks like to parent moment by moment. It's a choice of giving ourselves grace, choosing humility, thinking hopeful thoughts, praying before taking action, and relying on the Holy Spirit to fill in the gaps when we fall short.

We can continually redirect our words, thoughts, actions by asking ourselves:

At this moment, am I giving the love I would want to receive in my response, tone, words, and actions?

_____
_____
_____
_____
_____
_____
_____

As a parent, thinking about my children, am I someone I would want to hang out with?

_____
_____
_____
_____
_____
_____

If my answer is "no," how can I make changes to be a parent who is enjoyable to be with?

_____

_____

_____

_____

_____

_____

"He gives strength to the weary, And to him who has no might He increases power. Even youths grow weary and tired, And vigorous young men stumble badly, But those who wait for the Lord [who expect, look for, and hope in Him]
Will gain new strength and renew their power; They will lift up their wings [and rise up close to God] like eagles [rising toward the sun]; They will run and not become weary, They will walk and not grow tired." (Isaiah 40:29-31 AMP)

ADDITIONAL PARENTING ARTICLES

Writing is one of my favorite pastimes. When the craziness in our house slows, I get to sit in moments and think about what my kids are teaching me. Parenting is a continual gift of enjoying, cultivating, making adjustments, choosing love, growing, praying, laughing, forgiving, and so much more!

Each month I share parenting articles of what my teens, and the teenagers I have the honor of counseling, are continually teaching me about parenting. Each of these lessons is a gift I treasure! I hope you enjoy a few of my monthly parenting articles, included below.

To receive monthly parenting articles, subscribe at beccagunyon.com

THE BEST VERSION OF ME

Ask yourself, "What is the *best* version of me? How can I give this version of me to those I live with and see every day?"

For instance, the best version of you might have a kind tone, laugh often, set and keep healthy boundaries without getting frustrated, and is overall enjoyable to be with!

Don't we (as parents) want to be remembered as this version? As a mom of 5, I desperately want to get it right! I have a list of what I want my kids to remember me as. Although it's never too late to start developing thriving relationships, my kids' elementary, middle school, and high school years are forming our adult relationship. I want to be someone my kids want to hang out with, don't you?

We can ask ourselves, "Would I want to be parented by me? (Why or why not?)"

If the answer is, "No." What changes do I need to make to my tone, my words, the way I make them feel?

When I asked this question at a Parenting Workshop, one of the moms said, "It starts with who I am as a person and where I find my identity!" She is 100 percent right! It is impossible to give what we don't have. If we embrace the fact that we are seen as a "masterpiece" by the Creator of the Universe. It is much easier to give and live this truth to our kids. If we are constantly berating ourselves for where we don't measure up, it will come out in the way we treat everyone around us. Who we are to those around us is determined by our thoughts about ourselves and where we find our own identity.

Side Note: If you struggle with your identity, I can relate! That's my story: insecurity and anxiety. I didn't want to give this version of me to my kids. The heart of God and embracing and personalizing what the love of Jesus really means is life-changing. I would love to send you *Journey to His Heart* (A new book about embracing the heart of God so we can live it out). Contact me at beccagunyon.com for your copy.

Making changes feels overwhelming. You might think, "Is it worth it? Is it too late?"

At the grocery store recently, I saw a mom of one of the high school girls I counseled over 15 years ago. She gave me a big hug and said, "We thought we were bringing our daughter to you for you to fix her problems, and then you told my husband *he* needed to make changes…. he is so grateful and now they have a great relationship!"

As a young counselor, I remember being terrified to communicate this! Yet, this family taught me that knowing what our kids need is empowering and acting on it is the most important thing you can do as a parent. Making changes while our kids are still in our home is worth it, because it has a direct correlation on the adult relationships, we will have with each of them in the future.

Self-Reflection:

- Do I see myself as loved and treasured by God? If not, can I begin to see God as a Father who loves me and is for me?
- Am I being the best version of myself to those I live with?
- Am I willing to ask my spouse and kids what it feels like to be on the other side of me?
- After asking this question, am I willing to make changes based on the answers?

Prayer:

God, I invite You into every area of my life. Empower me to give love, joy, hope, and peace to those around me every day in my moments. I give You me. In Jesus name

"For we are His workmanship [His own master work, a work of art], created in Christ Jesus [reborn from above—spiritually transformed, renewed, ready to be used] for good works, which God prepared [for us] beforehand [taking paths which He set], so that we would walk in them [living the good life which He prearranged and made ready for us]." (Ephesians 2:10 AMP)

WHAT HAS HE CALLED ME TO DO TODAY?

Have you ever thought, "I just can't _____!" Me too!

Looking back, I can remember specifics at different stages when I thought,

- I can't... when all five kids (under age ten) had the stomach bug and messes were everywhere.
- I can't go on another trip to the emergency room because my preschooler can't breathe.
- I can't every time one of my kids asks me for help with math homework!
- I can't handle hearing my middle schooler's heartache so deep. It hurts too much!
- I can't be patient and calm as loud video games and music blare from a basement full of teenagers.
- I can't let them go, while waving and letting them drive off for the very first time.
- I can't embrace this new chapter of them growing up, while sitting in college orientation about to let her fly.

"I can't. I don't feel equipped. I don't want to."

We might find ourselves having this conversation with God in the privacy of our minds.

What is your "I can't...?"

This summer, I found a new translation of this popular verse:

"I can do all things (which He has called me to) through Him who strengthens and empowers me." (Philippians 4:13 AMP)

My "I can't" turned into asking God, "What are You calling me to do today?"

As a parent, this question will be answered differently at each stage of our child's life.

Newborn: We are called to be what our precious little one needs.

Infancy: We are called to snuggle, nurture, and feed our baby.

Baby: We are called to create safe spaces for crawling, walking, learning, and laughing.

Toddlers: We are called to hold a hand, discipline in love, explain so many elements of Creation.

Preschool: We are called to answer questions, teach them kind tones, and how to communicate.

Elementary School: We are called to help with school, teach kindness, create new boundaries.

Middle School: We are called to speak life, combatting insecurities, to look past reactions, and give encouragement.

High School: We are called to ask questions before giving advice and remind them what is most important.

College: We are called to encourage, be a safe place to come home to, to still be a parent, but also be a friend.

At Every Stage: We are called to pray and to be a reflection of the love, truth, and heart of Jesus. Thankfully, He will empower us to do this!

Sometimes His calling can seem mundane to us. The seemingly ordinary of each stage, like changing diapers, driving carpool, or helping with homework, can seem insignificant. Yet caring for our children is His calling on our life. That moment, that hour, that day, that stage has a lifetime of impact on our kids' lives.

Recently, my mentor spoke to my drivenness and said, "What is *most* important is the people you live with and giving care and love to each of them."

Every day, we can ask ourselves, "**What has He called me to do today?**"

I woke up to a text from my dear friend, Sarah Carroll, the day we were dropping off Addi at college, "You can do the hard thing!"

As I sat in her words I realized, "Yes, I can do the hard thing with His help, I might not *feel* ready or *feel* like I want to, but YES! I can embrace this new chapter joyfully!" Day by day, I am more and more aware that, when He calls us to do hard things, He empowers us with strength beyond our own comprehension and gives us His joy!

We CAN do what He is calling us to do. We can do the hard thing, because He will empower us, strengthen us, carry us, live through us, and walk beside us!

As parents, we want to get it right. We want to raise kids and teens that will become thriving adults and give life to the world around them. Our children long for tenderness, unconditional love, grace, boundaries, and a thriving relationship with us. Our relationship with our kids can be a gift to each of them, and to us. Our kids' ordinary moments can be EXTRAordinary by the way we interact with them at each stage!

Self-Reflection:

- What stage of parenting am I in?
- What is my favorite?
- What is my least favorite?
- How do I need God's help to make ordinary moments EXTRAordinrary?

Prayer:

"I can do _____ because You called me to. Please empower and strengthen me in Jesus name."

> *"I can do all things [which He has called me to do] through Him who strengthens and empowers me [to fulfill His purpose—I am self-sufficient in Christ's sufficiency; I am ready for anything and equal to anything through Him who infuses me with inner strength and confident peace.]" (Philippians 4:13 AMP)*

BUILDING OUR HOME

"Through skillful and godly Wisdom is a house (a life, a home, a family) built, and by understanding it is established [on a sound and good foundation], And by knowledge shall its chambers [of every area] be filled with all precious and pleasant riches." (Proverbs 24:3-4 AMPC)

Wisdom, understanding, and knowledge are the keys to equipping our children to grow up to be healthy adults in an unhealthy world. Every time I read this verse it stops me in my tracks. We all want wisdom, understanding, knowledge.

Technology, movies, and society communicate messages that contradict what we are trying to teach our kids and teens. Everything around us points to doing what *feels* right, even if it's not the actual right thing to do.

We may be asking ourselves:

- How do we teach our kids to do the right thing and live with honor?
- How do we equip our children to resist temptation?
- How do we instill in our children the love of God in a way that leads them to embrace Jesus and live out His love?
- How do we raise children who will unselfishly help others?

As parents, it would be amazing if we had ALL the answers for every situation.

"Fix these words of Mine on your hearts and minds; tie them as symbols on your hands and bind them on your foreheads. Teach them to your children, talking with them about them when you sit at home and when you walk

along the road when you lie down and when you get up. Write them on the doorframes of your house and your gates." (Deuteronomy 11:18-20)

God responds to my questions, "One day at a time, share Me and My Way with your children. Let Me be present in your house at all times, invite Me in by modeling and sharing that you can pray about everything."

I found a journal entry from 2010:

> As Dan and I sat with our kids doing our nightly devotion, I wish I could say that everyone was sitting at attention. Kids are all over the room in various places, one or two lying down, one snuggling with me, one keeps trying to crawl underneath the bed, and I have already stopped one of them from doing handstands. I am taken back to my childhood when my parents would share Jesus with my siblings and me. We would read a Bible story together, maybe sing a song, say a prayer, Dad might lead us in the Lord's prayer... then we would all go to our rooms and sleep peacefully. These are precious memories, I wanted to give this to my kids. This time with my family growing up was when I learned stories about Biblical characters, and life character qualities that were imprinted on my heart. I am trying to do this with my kids. Sometimes I think "I am so tired, maybe we'll skip it tonight." Sure, enough my three-year-old, who is stalling going to sleep, will say, "Mommy, are we gonna read the Bible story before bedtime?"

At different stages, family devo time will also look different. As parents, depending on what works for each family, we can set the routine. With Owin and Addi in college, and Eben in high school, our nightly routine is different. Now, we try to gather monthly to talk about Jesus and pray together (even if the older kids are on facetime). As three of our kids are older teens, we have chosen to let them own their spiritual development, faith and their relationship with Jesus. I still love time with my younger two sons—reading Bible stories at night and praying together.

Family time and sharing Jesus with one another makes Him real in a world that tries to leave Him out. Jesus can be a part of our everyday life so that our children see life through His eyes. In time and with repetition, this practice together gives us an unexpected gift, our kids grow closer in their sibling relationships as they grow in the relationship with God.

Self-Reflection:

- How can our family grow together in our walk with Jesus?
- Is this a priority for our family?
- If not, what changes can we make this year to spend time together growing in our faith?

Prayer:

God, show us how to create a home where Your wisdom, understanding and knowledge reign. May Your wisdom be the foundation my children base their life on. In Jesus name

"You shall teach them [diligently] to your [a] children [impressing God's precepts on their minds and penetrating their hearts with His truths], speaking of them when you sit in your house and when you walk along the road and when you lie down and when you rise up." (Deuteronomy 11:10 AMP)

THE PLAN IS GOOD

"'For I know the plans I have for you,' declares the Lord, 'plans to prosper you and not to harm you, plans to give you hope and a future. Then you will call on me and come and pray to me, and I will listen to you. You will seek me and find me when you seek me with all your heart.'" (Jeremiah 29:11-13 NIV)

In the noise, God whispers His Words in our thoughts.

Sometimes the swirl of life around me is just so loud. You can probably relate to the noise. What is your house like?

Here are a few of the noises in our home: alarms go off at all different times from 6:00 to 8:00 a.m., the dog barks loudly at a neighbor walking by, kids are leaving for school, zoom calls start, teens are leaving to workout, breakfast routines are starting, my husband is talking in a meeting with a headset. As if mornings weren't loud enough on their own, when I scroll through my phone, messages are loud and, at times, mean, I am saddened by the barrage of news posts or captured by the smiles on social media tempting me to enter the comparison trap.

If I choose to, I can silence the noise. Listen to His truth and let truth create in me who I want to be for my kids.

Before all of the craziness of our day begins, God wakes me up with a verse. Hearing Scripture echo in my mind is how God reminds me of what I need to choose to think about. This verse replays in my mind, when life felt confusing.

Now this verse has become a constant reminder, "*I know the plan for (you, each of your children/teens) and the plan is good.*"

"*For* I (God) *know...*" This in itself brings comfort. Something about God knowing what is going on in our home, with my kids, and in my heart brings peace.

"*For I know*" life is hard.

"*For I know*" America feels messy.

"*For I know*" how challenging it is to help teens understand truths.

"*For I know*" there is disappointment everywhere.

"*For I know*" exactly how you feel.

"*For I know*" tomorrow when you are confused by today.

Plans to Prosper

God knows the plan for each of us and the plan is GOOD! He has plans to prosper us in a broken world, even when life keeps changing or bringing disappointment.

Personalizing and thinking about this verse with each of my kids creates hope.

- "*I have plans to prosper*" your older two (as they move to the next stage: college, sports, work).
- "*I have plans to prosper*" your teen (who is struggling emotionally with disappointment).
- "*I have plans to prosper*" your child (who struggles academically).

- *"I have plans to prosper"* your middle school student (who is dealing with rejection, sadness, loneliness).
- *"I have plans to prosper"* your teen (who is struggling with temptation).
- *"I have plans to prosper"* your child (who is a dreamer and feels a little hopeless).
- *"I have plans to prosper"* you (as a parent choosing to pray about all your worries).

Seeking His Heart

When I believe His heart and His plans are good, my thoughts look to Him and not to life's circumstances. This transforms hopelessness into hopefulness. Seeking His heart and finding solace there rescues me from negativity and worry. He knows the plan and the plan is good, because He is good. He is loving, He is for everyone I care for, and for me.

Letting this truth settle in the depths of my soul brings life. When I choose to believe that He is good, regardless of how life feels, I want to go to Him, to cling to Him. I want to seek Him, I want to pray to Him, I want to crawl up in His arms, a safe place for me (and you).

> *"Then you will call on me and come and pray to me, and I will listen to you. You will seek me and find me when you seek me with all your heart." (Jeremiah 29:12-13)*

As you personalize this verse what would you insert?

For He knows _____ (how I feel, think, worry).

He knows the plan for _____ (me, my children, my husband, my need) and the plan is good.

Self-Reflection:

- How can I seek God today (in prayer, through His Word, thinking about Him, finding a quiet place to journal)?
- What worry can I give to Him in prayer?

Prayer:

God, I give You _____ (the things that swirl in my head about each child, my worries about the future, my anxiety about job things, my frustration with my family). I know Your heart and plan are good. Give me strength to trust You in the difficult moments. I choose to trust Your plan to prosper my family. Give us hope, joy, peace, and love as we live our moments trusting You. In Jesus name

CREATING A ROUTINE OF THANKFULNESS

"Summing it all up, friends, I'd say you'll do best by filling your minds and meditating on things true, noble, reputable, authentic, compelling, gracious—the best, not the worst; the beautiful, not the ugly; things to praise, not things to curse." (Philippians 4:8 MSG)

Our thoughts become our life; we live out our thoughts!

As parents, one of our most important roles is to help shape our kids' thought life! We are shaping our kids' thoughts, framing, and perspective in seemingly ordinary moments—whether we realize it or not.

We all want the best life for our kids, don't we? We desire life to the FULL for them. How can we give this gift to our kids?

"Jesus said, 'The thief comes only in order to steal and kill and destroy. I came that they may have and enjoy life, and have it in abundance [to the full, till it overflows].'" (John 10:10 AMP)

Thoughts lead to feelings, emotions, and behaviors, which guides our actions.

This principle was taught in one of my first counseling classes, and out of all the classes I took, this principle speaks to me more than any of the others. For instance, we can ask ourselves, "What am I thinking about right now? How does this thought affect me?"

Our thoughts about our life (family members, the future, church, work, politics, coworkers, friends, yesterday, future, God...) are influencing the way we feel, the way we are interacting with others, and our attitude about everything.

Our thoughts are fueling or frustrating every aspect of our lives!

When I counsel students, my hope is to help guide each teen I walk beside to think thankful, hopeful, grateful, life-giving thoughts! Changing our thinking, one thought at a time, is key in healing from anxiety, anger, self-hate, depression, past pain, or rejection.

Every single one of us, including our kids, chooses our own thought! Our children and teens need to know this truth, our thoughts determine so many aspects of the quality of our life!

The private conversations we have in our mind can be life-giving instead of draining or self-deprecating. Very few thoughts are neutral. Thinking great can lead us to our best life while negative and self-defeating thoughts can lead to destruction and even depression. We can't force our kids or teens to think differently, they must choose their own thoughts. As a parent, this truth can be a bit overwhelming. Yet, we can give our kids and teens tools that will shape their thinking. We can also model thinking thankful by daily talking about what we are grateful for.

"If you realized how powerful your thoughts are, you would never think a negative thought." (Leaf, 2007).

The first step to changing our thought life is identifying how powerful each thought is, and that negative and self-defeating thoughts are destructive!

Questions to ask ourselves are: "What needs to change in my thought patterns? What can I as a parent do to help shape my kids' thoughts?"

We can start by thinking thankful ourselves—modeling waking up and thinking great is contagious.

With my own kids, and as a counselor, I knew I couldn't change their thoughts for them. So, I came up with a simple, practical, routine that, if repeated, could change thoughts, which leads to changes in the brain, which changes emotions, which leads to a great life!

Choose Life to the Fullest Routine:

1. Wake up every morning and write five "thankfuls" (things I enjoy).
2. Read Scripture and ask self-reflective questions.
3. Say a prayer, "Jesus, I invite You into my thoughts, my life, my moments, my stress, my feelings, my worries, my friendships, my struggles…"
4. Ask myself, "Who can I give life to today?"

After 120 days of this routine, I watched a miracle happen in my own home with my teenage son. We can help our kids think great! This shift doesn't happen overnight, however, choosing to think thankful changes emotional, mental, and even physical health.

So much of life is what we think about it. When we choose life-giving thoughts, we are transforming our brain to think the "best, not the worst."

In my ministry experience, every single growth area has been birthed in brokenness. This idea for creating a routine of choosing life to the fullest began in a place of helplessness.

Here is the backstory for *Choose Life to the Fullest*:

Several years ago, one of my teens was filled with self-hate, negativity, and depression. His thoughts were constantly spiraling into unhealthy places. Nothing was working, I felt overwhelmed by his pain… I faced a hard reality.

I could not *make* my teenage clients or even my own teenager choose to think differently! Thinking involves a personal choice.

Reading Caroline Leaf's book, *Switch On Your Brain,* further convinced me of how every thought shapes the brain, so what could I do?

"How we think not only affects our own spirit, soul, and body but also people around us." (Leaf, 2007)

Knowing this Scripture principle of 2 Corinthians 10:5 *"...and we are taking every thought and purpose captive to the obedience of Christ."* the truth hit hard. I knew how imperative it was to help my kids realize their own choice and the benefit of thinking life-giving!

I asked myself lots of questions. How could I help my son want to choose to think better, healthier, more grateful? If he made the choice, where could he start creating new thought patterns? What would motivate him to start a new thinking routine?

Growing up, my best friends were my pastor's daughters. I learned a lot about motivating teens to grow spiritually, their dad paid them to read the Bible. So, I had a thought, I could write daily posts for students on Instagram and pay my son to edit them!

Taking Scripture and brain research seriously, I knew this daily routine, of writing his "thankfuls," reading Scripture, asking self-reflective questions, inviting Jesus into every area of his life, and looking around to see who he could help would lead to life change.

Daily, I wrote thought devotionals for him to edit. He started proofreading each post for $2 a day. He read for 30 days. At 60 days he was still reading. 90 days he was still reading. About 120 days in, he walked into the kitchen one morning and casually said, "Mom, I like myself."

Trying to hide my excitement and shock, I continued scrambling eggs as happy tears started flowing. I knew God had done a miracle, because, over time, waking up thinking thankful and growing in our faith journey changes the way we see ourselves. Walking with Jesus and inviting Him in creates transformation!

Anyone can do this routine!

My posts becoming books was not my plan, publishing wasn't even a thought. I just wanted my son and the teens I mentor to live life to the full! Because my son kept reading, I kept writing. One of my son's friends, who was reading them, asked me to publish and turn these daily devos into books. This led to the *Choose Life to the Fullest* series. Four books comprised of daily devotionals. The last book I wrote with my brother, Micah Owings, who played professional baseball. I love to give books to students and the teens I mentor, and my own kids read them. Each time one of my kids finish a book, I give them a gift card! Why? I figure if my pastor's daughters got paid to read the Bible as teens and still read their Bible 30 years later then this motivation method is ok! :)

I watched a miracle in my own home, and I continually thank God for this!

We can choose to live life to the FULL! (John 10:10)

Self-Reflection:

- What five things am I grateful for today?
- Who can I give life to today?

Prayer:

To create change, this simple discipline takes repetition. Our minds *can* be transformed by the love of Jesus. God's power and love is beyond comprehension, He can transform our minds. Throughout the day, we can say a simple powerful prayer: "Jesus, I invite You into my thoughts, emotions, fears, disappointment, situations, relationships, work, ministry, dreams, and goals. I give You me, transform my thoughts by Your tender powerful love."

".... the mind governed by the Spirit is life and peace." (Romans 8:6 NIV)

THE GIFT OF ADVERSITY

A few days ago, I watched a miracle as my adult child conquered adversity.

If you have a child who your heart has been broken for—who has experienced rejection, heartache, struggle—that you can, at times, physically feel the burdens your child wears, I can relate. I have worn knee pads out praying for this one, who continually chooses to work hard and make wise choices, and yet life just seems so difficult. Situations that "should" work out haven't. Rejection appears for no apparent reason. When I am tired, in my humanness, I ask God, "Why?"

Yet God knows what He is doing as He trains warriors. Years of perseverance through adversity have created solid character, an attitude of risk, an unwavering faith, and a tender heart for those who hurt.

Adversity doesn't feel like a gift when we are walking through it with our children and teens. Life can be cruel to one of our dear ones, our heart longs to rescue immediately. Rescuing could be the solution, or what love requires of us may be walking beside that child, training them for life's battles.

We are raising warriors, and warriors, even princess warriors, face adversity.

Adversity builds inner strength, which builds a foundation of solid, authentic character. Brave, noble, kind, tender, strong, hopeful, courageous, ready to risk, protective, and firm in their faith… This is the kind of warrior I want to raise. On those days when I think it would be easier to tell them not to risk, not to leap or to put themselves out there, we too must be brave. Watching our kids travel through adversity is difficult. As a parent raising warriors, it means that we must let go of our own fears, feelings, and desire for control and comfort. Living faith instead of fear will be our constant choice. The choice of faith shields us and those we love from the arrows of fear.

Courageously choosing each step to travel the road beside our kids allows our heart to enter their struggles. Love, tenderness, and truth all meet here. Here in this difficult and uncomfortable place we cultivate a relationship with a solid foundation that will remain secure.

Staying true to our goal of growing warriors to battle mediocrity, temptation, rejection, and life's trouble is the calling that can feel too big for a parent's heart. Yet, God will give us all that we need, for He handpicked us to raise the ones He entrusts us with. We can cling to His promises as we repeat them in a prayer:

> *"May the God of hope fill you with all joy and peace as you trust in him, so that you may overflow with hope by the power of the Holy Spirit."* In Jesus name *(Romans 15:13 NIV)*

As we fight our battles, prayer can be our lifeline, sustaining our heart while He intervenes. In our weariness, when we are wondering where He is, in His way and in His timing, He whispers hope. In time, His plan is revealed, deliverance, victory, and celebration will appear We will look back and see His presence guiding us and helping all of us travel adversity.

As parents we can choose to keep praying, keep loving, keep walking beside our warriors in training as we help build in them solid character, inner strength, and faith that will become perseverance. Walking beside our children and teens through difficult times is a road of honor that will bless us continually. Traveling adversity together can build a closeness that will stand the test of time, the stages of growth, and continually enrich our lives now and in the future!

Self-Reflection:

- What heartache, pain, or adversity am I facing?
- Can I give it to God?

Prayer:

God, I give You _____. It's hard to watch my kids walk through this. At times, I don't know what do to or say, so I need You to empower me and give me Your peace. Strengthen my child/teen and empower them with Your strength. May my children know Your heart for them is love. In Jesus name

"I have told you these things, so that in Me you may have [perfect] peace. In the world you have tribulation and distress and suffering, but be courageous [be confident, be undaunted, be filled with joy]; I have overcome the world."
[My conquest is accomplished, My victory abiding.]" (John 16:33 AMP)

I LOVED BEING HERE

What are your favorite memories growing up? Recently, my siblings came to watch my youngest, Anden, pitch at a field next to the same field where I watched my brothers in high school. Lots of favorite Owings ballpark memories flooded my mind. I kept flashing back to hot spring days, pregnant at this same ballpark almost twenty years ago. Now I am surrounded by my husband, siblings, and parents, and my own five kids and my nephews.

The ballpark has always been a place that brings our family closer together, and there is a reason behind this. My parents, Jim and Danise Owings, cultivated the culture of enjoying sports together. Many years ago, my mom gave Dan and I the most amazing advice when our oldest, Owin, was in T-ball.

"It's the hug after the game—this is the most important!"

She went on to say, "Whether there is a homerun or a strikeout, don't act too excited, and don't ever appear angry. Always use the same verbiage. Do not let your kids think their performance affects your happiness or how proud you are of them."

After every game or performance, she said, "I loved watching you play! I loved being here!"

My parents lived this! The attitude after the game was always a feeling of fun and excitement, everyone loved getting to be there, just to watch each other play! As I flashback to fields all across the country at every level of this game,

I can hear my dad's warm laugh, regardless of the outcome, and remember enjoying a meal together after the game.

There were definitely meals where my siblings or I were upset about our own performance. Sports can be hard on the heart. Most kids wrestle with insecurities, performance, expectations, failure… However, my parents did not add to the frustration we were already feeling. When the time was right, they helped us work through our emotions and keep going.

As parents, we can choose our reaction, our timing and our tone!

Leaving the field, I heard two dads from another team with their sons.

One dad said, "You should have…." His tone was angry. His son's head was down. I wouldn't have wanted to go home with this guy, would you?

The dad a few steps behind him said to his son, "In the second game what are three things you did well?" His tone was calm. He was comforting his son. This was probably a much better car ride home. He chose to focus on the positives! He is teaching his son a valuable lesson.

Most kids already know about the error they made—the ball they could have caught, the strikeout that could have been a hit, the pitch they threw down the middle, the missed goal, the bad serve, the fumble, the forgotten lines in the play, the missed music note… they're already berating themselves. Why add our voice to their inner critic? It only leads to resentment, shutting down, anger, and shame, making it more difficult to bounce back from a disappointment.

Our kids need to believe their performance does not affect our emotions. If their performance affects our happiness this causes too much pressure.

It's the hug after the game, the "I loved watching you play!" We want to create great memories with our kids! The ballpark has always brought my family together. Lots of cheers, laughter, overcoming adversity, and facing failure abound on the field, so much takes place at sporting events. This place has always brought us closer because of the culture created by Pop and Noni.

Here's what they taught us:

- It's the hug after the game that is important!
- Always say, "I loved being here, I loved watching you play."
- Resist the temptation to lecture on the ride home, the relationship is more important than performance. So, choose to wait and think before we speak.
- Don't let your kids' performance affect your emotions.

Self-Reflection:

- Does my kids' performance affect me? How?
- What do I do or say after sporting events, competitions, or performances?
- Is the way I react strengthening or hurting my relationship with my children?
- After an event, game, match, etc. what is the car ride home like?

Prayer:

God, I need to change _____. I need Your help. Please forgive me for focusing on performance instead of the person. Please mend relationships in my family. Remind me throughout each event or game my children perform or play in that I can choose to stay calm and enjoy being there, because I love the child/teen You entrusted me with. In Jesus name.

"This is My commandment, that you love and unselfishly seek the best for one another, just as I have loved you...You have not chosen Me, but I have chosen you and I have appointed and placed and purposefully planted you, so that

you would go and bear fruit and keep on bearing, and that your fruit will remain and be lasting, so that whatever you ask of the Father in My name [as My representative] He may give to you. This [is what] I command you: that you love and unselfishly seek the best for one another." (John 15:12-17 AMP)

WOULD I WANT TO BE PARENTED BY ME?

When my kids were little, I was given the gift of seeing different parenting styles through the eyes of teens I counseled. Some of them had enjoyable relationships with their parents, while others were angry and resentful. With every student, I saw a common theme: **EVERY teen desires an authentic relationship with each of their parents.**

Even the healthiest relationships require communicating and, sometimes, apologizing. The messier relationships took time, breaking down walls and building bridges, apologizing and making changes. When steps toward relational healing happened—the teens' hearts would follow their parents' choice to change.

Secretly, each teen was hoping for this… to have a healthy relationship with each of their parents. This happened in my own home with one of mine. That is our backstory, which created a passion for helping parents connect with their kids/teens and creating the best possible relationship.

Transformation is possible! God makes miracles out of messes!

Self-evaluation is life-giving, courageous, and difficult, but facing reality can lead to a decision to take steps toward transformation!

To kickstart our steps toward positive transformation, we can ask ourselves, "Am I willing to make the necessary changes to have a healthy relationship with my child?

Simple and practical changes can be made by reflecting on 1 Corinthians 13:

- Am I patient (in the way I respond)?
- Am I kind (in the way I react)?
- Am I thoughtful? (Do I put myself in my kids' shoes?)
- Am I prideful? (Or am I willing to humbly say, "I'm sorry.")
- Am I easily angered? (If so, are my kids following me in this?)
- Do I focus on the best qualities in those I live with? (Or do I focus on the things that annoy me?)
- Do I give my kids hope even when they continue to struggle?
- Do I believe the best about those around me?
- What changes does love require of me?
- What is one way I can live love with my kids today?

"Love endures with patience and serenity, love is kind and thoughtful, and is not jealous or envious; love does not brag and is not proud or arrogant. It is not rude; it is not self-seeking, it is not provoked [nor overly sensitive and easily angered]; it does not take into account a wrong endured. It does not rejoice at injustice, but rejoices with the truth [when right and truth prevail]. Love bears all things [regardless of what comes], believes all things [looking for the best in each one], hopes all things [remaining steadfast during difficult times], endures all things [without weakening]. Love never fails [it never fades nor ends]." 1 Corinthians 13 (AMP)

If we live in the unconditional, tender love of Jesus, we will have enough love to overflow into our relationships with our kids. God, in His goodness, chose us to parent each of our children and teens. Therefore, He will equip us. We can continually ask Him for patience, kindness, joy, laughter, wisdom, and understanding as we live love!

Self-Reflection:

- Would I want to be parented by me?
- If not, what changes does love require of me?
- Do I believe the best about those around me?
- What is one way I can live love with my kids today?

Prayer:

Jesus, I choose to embrace, accept, and live in Your love. Fill my heart with Your love so that it spills out on my family. Thank You that Your love never fails.

"Love never fails [it never fades nor ends]." (1 Corinthians 13: 4-8 AMP)

SEASON OF LAUNCHING

Every moment is a gift to treasure! Even in the season of launching!

Earlier this summer, I shared with my dear college friend, Courtney Rue, how hard it is to let our kids fly. She sent me this message:

> You raise your kids and pour into them, and sometime around high school graduation you realize they have become your very favorite people. Your favorite people to hang out with, laugh with, and have adventures with. And just about that same time, you have to launch them off into the world. Your child becomes this amazing person you want to be with all the time—and then they leave. It feels terribly unfair! But I guess that is part of the nature of motherhood. Our children are a gift we give to the world. Don't fret too much, they do return to their mamas often, via phone calls, text and FaceTime, seeking us out. Which is the BEST thing ever!

All summer, maybe all year, I have been in a bit of a fog. The reality of launching one child and then another the next year has hit. I have been trying to wrap my arms around what life will look like every day after they fly, and yet still enjoy every moment!

Time flies so quickly!

As the oldest of five children, I watched my little brothers grow up. JonMark is ten years younger than me. When he was a baby, my mom let me rock him to sleep on a daily basis. When I was a junior in high school, Micah and JonMark were six and eight, I remember tucking them in at night, taking them to baseball lessons, getting ice cream together, little league games, helping with homework and birthday parties, prom pictures, graduation, and then one day I looked over and they were men.

When my oldest, Owin, was born, I had already seen how fast childhood flies, and I knew moments are to be treasured. A childhood is made up of little moments. How our kids remember us is dependent on how we live our moments.

This summer, I have been holding on to moments a little bit longer as the reality of launching hit me. We launched our oldest last year, then our daughter this year, in two years another son will be launched and eventually two more sons will fly.

Our oldest two will leave for college in a few weeks. Everything will look different around here—the daily routines, the dinner table, the atmosphere of our home.

All summer Courtney's words have echoed in my mind, reminding me that these feelings I have are normal. Through all of this, I am also realizing that in this next season we can get closer as a family and our relationship still grow in depth.

During Owin's freshman year, we talked on the phone often, he facetimed me weekly when he was in the batting cage, and he came home for Thanksgiving and Christmas break and summer. At first, launching him felt so final, but as the year went on it simply became a new chapter—walking beside our adult son.

Watching our kids fly has another emotion too, this element of excitement and being so very proud of the person they are becoming!

Self-Reflection:

- How am I living my moments?
- Am I in a season of parenting that is hard to accept?
- How can I embrace this chapter with each of my kids?

Prayer:

Jesus, I give You me. Help me to embrace this season. Empower me with Your strength. In Jesus name

> *"Strength and dignity are her clothing, and her position is strong and secure; And she smiles at the future [knowing that she and her family are prepared]." (Proverbs 31:25 AMP)*

ENTRUSTING

Earlier this week, I dreamed our family (my husband, Dan, my kids, Owin (age 20), Addi (18), Eben (16), JohnE (14), Anden (11) entered a train terminal.

Funnily enough, every train looked like a school bus. I heard the overhead announcement saying loudly, "Pick your bus, it will deliver you to your destination, at roller coaster speeds."

Roller coaster speeds…what? Twenty years ago, I loved roller coasters, but now I felt nervous, not sure what to expect.

Owin had already found his train/bus, Addi jumped on another bus, I couldn't find Eben or JohnE, Dan, Anden, and I got on one bus, sat down, and then we got off. I couldn't pick a bus. I couldn't get everyone together, I felt confused, alarmed, and a little lost.

Addi looked at me from her bus with those big blue eyes and mouthed, "Mom, I'm good!"

Immediately, all the trains/buses took off at rocket speed! Dan, Anden, and I were left watching. On the inside I was panicking, because in the chaos, I couldn't find JohnE or Eben. Where did their bus/train go? I felt lost. Trying to wrap my arms around everyone going different directions, I stood there staring, shocked…

What just happened? Where did time go?

Waking up from this odd dream, I couldn't go back to sleep. My mind was whirring. Life is moving really fast. I know my college kids are going where God is leading them, yet there are so many unknowns. Eben got his driver's license this week. How much freedom should I give him? And JohnE, I wonder what adventure God has for him this year? And how can we help Anden have the same adventures and experiences his older siblings had?

Earlier this week, Addi and I were walking and discussing unknowns and what tomorrow holds. She gently reminded me, "If you are too focused on the future, you can't live in the present." She has a way of speaking truth. Her voice was God's way of reminding me to embrace all my moments without putting up a protective stance or choosing to live anxious.

She is right, I should enjoy today… but how? I liked yesterday and I can't wrap my brain or heart around tomorrow.

My heart whispered, "Live today well, live loving this moment, live life to the full with everyone in your home! Give God tomorrow."

This is a new chapter, I do want to learn to embrace it, yet I loved yesterday's chapter. Days when we are all together, nights (when at some point) all my kids would be home in their own bed, moments when all five kids are in the car together, laughing, joking, even picking at each other. I loved this chapter. Am I ready for it to be over?

Yet, the page is turning…

How do I enjoy today when I am nervous and anxious, or I can't wrap my head around my new normal? In this chapter there are so many unknowns.

God whispered to my heart, *"Entrust each child into my care, I will take care of them, and I will also take care of your heart."*

My heart knows entrusting is my only choice to be the best version of me to those I love.

How do I entrust my children, teens, and college kids into His care?

Years ago, I found this verse, Acts 20:32. An unexplainable peace settles over my soul daily as I place each of my children's names in this verse.

Owin, Addi, Eben, JohnE, Anden, *"I commit you to God [I deposit you in His charge, entrusting you to His protection and care]. And I commend you to the Word of His grace [to the commands and counsels and promises of His unmerited favor]. It is able to build you up and to give you [your rightful] inheritance among all God's set-apart ones (those consecrated, purified, and transformed of soul)."* In Jesus name *(Acts 20:32 AMPC)*

If you are like me and you are in a new chapter of letting go, giving more freedom, or launching, there are so many unknowns. And although childhood moments together lead to launching and enjoying adult children, it can be difficult to wrap our arms and heart around.

Even though there might still be tears as we embrace new chapters, we can daily entrust each child into His care. Living entrusting leads to giving the best version of ourselves to those we love, as we bravely embrace new chapters, and living life to the FULL!

Self-Reflection:

- What does this season of "launching" look like?
- How do I entrust my children, teens, and college kids into His care?

Prayer:

"I commit you _____ (my child's name) *to God [I deposit you in His charge, entrusting you to His protection and care]. And I commend you to the Word of His grace [to the commands and counsels and promises of His unmerited favor]. It is able to build you up and to give you [your rightful] inheritance among all God's set-apart ones (those consecrated, purified, and transformed of soul)."* In Jesus name *(Acts 20:32 AMPC)*

WHAT CAN I DO?

"Are you tired? Worn out? … Come to me. Get away with me and you'll recover your life. I'll show you how to take a real rest. Walk with me and work with me—watch how I do it. Learn the unforced rhythms of grace. I won't lay anything heavy or ill-fitting on you. Keep company with me and you'll learn to live freely and lightly." (Matthew 11:28-30 MSG)

Sometimes I hear God's whisper, *"Are you tired? Learn the unforced rhythms of grace…"*

What does that even mean?

Most of us have a propensity inside of us to teach, prepare, instill, give, model, and equip our kids and teens with everything they need to be successful in life before they graduate, or maybe even before kindergarten.

We question ourselves: Am I doing enough? Do I have what it takes? How will they turn out?

Whether we realize it or not these thoughts drain us. If we add in the day-to-day responsibilities of school, work, sports, church/ministry, we will feel worn out. This question is one of my favorites, "What can I do right now in this moment?"

Let me backup, we can ask ourselves so many questions about the "how to's." I don't know how we are going lead our kids to finish all the assignments, make the team, have a great friend group in every season of life, get into the right college, marry an amazing spouse…Yet, what CAN I do?

What our kids will remember is how we make them feel by our tone, actions, words, and attitude about them and our life.

Instead of trying to get everything right down the road, focus on what can I do in this moment?

- I can choose an inviting tone. The tone we choose either enriches or stops the conversation with our kids and teens.
- I can pick one aspect of my child/teen's life to continually encourage. We can say: I love how you lead, I love your voice, I see your hard work, I am so proud of who you are, I love how you serve, I saw how kindly you responded in that situation. When we affirm something, we see in our kids they will grow in the area we encourage them in.
- I can speak life and hope saying, "God loves you and has amazing things for you!"
- I can pray that God meets every need our child, teen, and adult children have. *"And my God will liberally supply (fill until full) your every need according to His riches in glory in Christ Jesus." (Philippians 4:19 AMP)*
- I can make ordinary moments EXTRAordinary by the way I treat my kids! Ordinary moments (in the car, getting ready for school, doing schoolwork, cleaning) can become EXTRAORDINARY as we grow in relationship together!
- I can resist the urge to be grumpy, tired, or aloof and instead I can be excited to see each of my kids every day. I get to choose whether I act in my feelings or emotions or not.

I haven't met a single person who feels like they have figured every aspect of parenting out! As we surrender our parenting and our children to Him, God in His goodness pours grace, joy, love, healing, and laughter on our relationships enriching them, growing them, creating healing, and blessing our tomorrow!

Self-Reflection:

- What am I overwhelmed by or stressed about?
- What is the phrase or verse you can speak into your child or teen's life?
- What can I do today? (Make a list.)

Prayer:

God, I give You every aspect of my life (my thoughts, my feelings, my relationships, the way I care for each of my kids). Show me what I can do today. Shine through me. I want to live my moments with You. I want seemingly ordinary moment with my kids to be Extraordinary. Remind me of You and Your love throughout each day, so that I can give Your love to those around me. In Jesus name

> *"Get away with me and you'll recover your life. I'll show*
> *you how to take a real rest. Walk with me and work with*
> *me—watch how I do it." (Matthew 11:28 MSG)*

CONCLUSION

"Fix these words of mine on your hearts and minds; tie them as symbols on your hands and bind them on your foreheads. Teach them to your children, talking with them about them when you sit at home and when you walk along the road when you lie down and when you get up. Write them on the doorframes of your house and your gates." (Deuteronomy 11:18-20)

Daily my "go to" one liner prayer is "Jesus, please give each of my children *"resolute hearts"* for You." (Acts 11:23 NAS)

As parents, we want to get it right. Questions constantly confront me, "Am I doing enough? Am I missing anything? How do I balance or juggle all of the aspects of life, hats I wear, and things He has entrusted me with?"

God responds to my questions saying, "One day at a time, share Me and My Way with your children. One day at a time, let Me be present in your house at all times. One day at a time, invite Me in by modeling and sharing that you can pray about everything. Moment by moment model My love, share My joy, live My peace, be My comfort, invite Me into the day to day, live in relationship with Me, talk to Me about everything, and your children will see Me as the foundation of life." *"Remain in Me."* (John 15:4 AMP)

I truly believe God bends His ear to a parents' requests for their children and intervenes in ways only He can. We continually cultivate and He makes our children's lives "rooted in love" and bloom for His purposes. May each of us rest in knowing, as we entrust our children into His care He will do "immeasurably more than we can ask or imagine in their lives."

> *"Now to Him who is able to [carry out His purpose and] do superabundantly more than all that we dare ask or think [infinitely beyond our greatest prayers, hopes, or dreams], according to His power that is at work within us." (Ephesians 3:20 AMP)*

AUTHOR'S NOTE

One of the greatest gifts God has entrusted me and Dan with is our five children. We treasure Owin, Addi, Eben, JohnE, and Anden. Every moment is a gift, even though every moment is not always easy or happy!

I love our adventures to the beach and amusement parks, yet, somewhere in the midst of life with my five, I realized the everyday, the seemingly ordinary, even the possibly mundane moments are my favorite with my kids.

My heart smiles:

- When Owin (age 20) asks me to run an errand with him.
- When Addi (age 18) writes me a beautiful letter full of colors or helps me make dinner.
- When Eben (age 16) talks to me at midnight—the time that he is the most expressive.
- When JohnE (age 14) tells me jokes, talks in different accents, or asks me about middle school life.
- When Anden (age 11) wants to play catch or read a book together.
- When Dan and I pray together for our kids.

I love reflecting on moments where we did everyday things at each stage together. Creating a culture where we enjoy one another was a lot of work when they were little, yet every moment of caring and shaping continues to be worth it. Sometimes we had to make changes, apologize, totally change the course, seek advice, and Dan and I were/are constantly learning to work together better.

Self-reflection in each relationship with my kids, being willing to shift the way I am doing or saying things, and inviting Jesus in, though not always easy, is building relationships I daily enjoy! My hope and prayer for this book is that you discover the culture you want to cultivate and enjoy your moments cultivating. May God bless your home abundantly!

As parents, we can make seemingly ordinary moments EXTRAordinary by the way we live life together!

REFERENCES

Leaf, C. (2007). *Switch on your brain: the Key to peak happiness, thinking, and health.* Grand Rapids, MI: Baker Books.

Newberry, T. (2007) *The 4:8 principle: The secret to a joy-filled life.* Carol Stream, IL: Tyndale House.

Choose Life to the Fullest (books 1-3)

We are given the opportunity to choose to live our best life. We live out our thoughts. Each book contains 90 days of devotionals for creating a habit of thinking great and inviting Jesus in. These books were written with students in mind and are perfect for those starting a daily devotion routine.

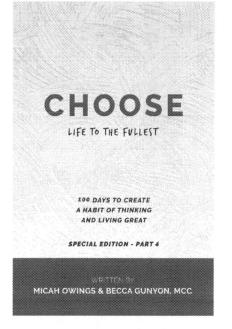

Choose Life to the Fullest Special Edition

This book was coauthored with my brother, Micah Owings, who played MLB for six years. He shares personal stories about his faith and how this was essential to his game. This book has the same format as the first three, yet adds a perspective of a dreamer, athlete, and go-getter. Choosing to think great is essential to reaching our goals. Developing a relationship with Jesus leads to living life to the full. (John 10:10)

The Treasure- Living Immersed in His Love

God has an ocean of love for all of us. We can live immersed in His love. While sharing simplistic imagery to explain growing in relationship with God, this book provides practical steps to take to embracing His love through a relationship with Jesus. This book contains three sections: The Treasure, Living Treasured, and Treasuring Others.

Visit beccagunyon.com for more information on speaking, seminars, and Parenting Moment by Moment.

Journey to His Heart is an adventure of personalizing Scripture to grow in depth in your relationship with Jesus. "His heart never runs out of love. His love is not determined by what she does or doesn't do. His love is big enough to cover insecurities and failures and dissolve them in His grace. In this place, she understood the foundation of His love."

Printed in the United States
by Baker & Taylor Publisher Services